Orton Gillingham Decodable 3rd Grade Readers

Easy decodable texts to improve reading and writing skills
in struggling readers and kids with dyslexia

Volume 3

BrainChild

Introduction

Teaching a child with dyslexia to read: Dyslexia is a specific and persistent learning disability that affects reading and writing. For children with dyslexia, learning to read and write can be a difficult challenge for families and educators to tackle. For these children, written language becomes a great barrier, often without meaning or logic, which generates rejection of the task, frustration and discomfort.

The child with dyslexia is a child who has significant difficulties in reading and writing, because their brain processes information differently than other children; which is why if we expect the same results following the traditional method, we will find many barriers that can and often do harm the child. It is important to become aware of the characteristics of this difficulty, so as to help the child learn to read and the consequent overcoming of their difficulties such as understanding, knowledge and attention to their needs.

Reading difficulties with dyslexia

Dyslexia is a learning disability of neurobiological origin, which causes seem to be in the maturation and structuring of certain brain structures.

Dyslexia is therefore a condition of the brain which causes it to process information differently, making it difficult for the person to understand letters, their sounds, their combinations, etc.

Human language is a language based on signs, letters, and their sounds, which are arbitrary. The correspondence of each grapheme (letter) with its phoneme (sound), does not follow any logic; it's simply chance. This is one of the greatest difficulties that children face when they must learn to read and write. Converting the spoken language, they know into signs and transforming sounds into letters is a challenge.

This is even more complicated in children with dyslexia; the relationship becomes something indecipherable for them. No matter how hard they try, they cannot make sense of that dance between letters and sounds. Children with dyslexia have a lot of difficulty recognizing letters; sometimes they mistake letters for others, write them backwards, etc.

Another difficulty they face, is knowing the sound that corresponds to each letter; and things get even more complicated when we combine several letters, and we have to know several sounds.

New words are a challenge for them, and they can forget them easily, so they must work hard to acquire them. Sometimes they read certain words effortlessly, but the next day they completely forget them.

When they write, they omit letters, change their position, forget words in a sentence, etc.

Dyslexia also affects reading comprehension. When they read, they are trying really hard to decipher and understand each word, sometimes even each letter; that is why the meaning of the text gets lost.

Reading comprehension: Activities to help develop it in children.

How to teach a child with dyslexia to read

A child with dyslexia has difficulty learning to read and write, because it is hard for them to recognize letters and know which sound, they correspond to. However, the child can learn to read and write and overcome those difficulties.

Remember that dyslexia is a learning difficulty that does not imply any physical or mental handicap; the child with dyslexia has adequate capacities. To teach a child with dyslexia to read, it is essential to know the nature of their difficulties, understand them and use a teaching method that responds to their needs.

A child with dyslexia

A teaching method to help a child with dyslexia read.

In the first place, it is necessary to assess the child, to know their reading and writing level, the nature and characteristics of their difficulties in order to understand their specific needs. For this, it is advisable to seek a specialist.

Reading favors the development of phonological awareness (which consists of the correspondence of the sound with the letter). To do this, start with simple activities, letter by letter. Even if other children around the same age read full texts, it may be necessary to start working letter by letter. Later, we can continue with the words, phrases and texts. It is about dedicating more time and more detail to the learning process.

Phonological awareness worksheets

Use motivational activities that are engaging. Do not limit the child to just paper and pencil: they can make letters out of play dough, write on sand with their fingers, play catch or games such as hangman, word searches, crossword puzzles, etc.
Don't force them to read or read a lot. Try to have them read on a daily basis, little by little; sometimes a sentence or a paragraph is enough. Help them understand what they read, ask them questions, ask them to read again, etc.

TABLE OF CONTENTS

The family tree

As soon as Emma heard that her social studies project was on creating a family tree, she couldn't wait to get started. She loved learning about history and discovering more about her roots, and this was the perfect opportunity to do just that.

Emma began by interviewing her parents and grandparents about their ancestors. Her parents told her about their great-grandparents who had emigrated from Europe to start a new life in America. Her grandparents shared stories of their own childhoods and the hardships they faced during the Great Depression.

Emma's curiosity grew with each conversation, and she delved deeper into her past. She searched online for public records and scanned old photo albums, piecing together her family tree one branch at a time.

As she worked on her project, Emma discovered fascinating stories about her ancestors - stories of bravery, resilience, and determination. She learned that her great-great-grandfather had fought in World War I, that her great-grandmother had been a suffragette, and that her grandfather had served in the Korean War.

Emma was amazed at how much she had discovered through this project. She felt like a detective, uncovering secrets, and solving mysteries. But what she enjoyed most were the connections she made between the people on her family tree.

She realized that her family was a patchwork quilt of different cultures, traditions, and experiences. She felt proud of the diversity in her family and the different paths that her relatives had taken. Emma knew that these stories would continue to be passed down and woven into the fabric of her family's identity.

When Emma presented her family tree to her class, her teacher was impressed by the amount of detail and effort she had put into the project. Emma was proud to share her findings with her classmates, and even more proud to share the stories of her ancestors.

The project had given Emma a new appreciation for her family and where she came from. She knew that she would continue to explore her family's history and learn more about the people who had come before her.

As she looked at the completed family tree, Emma felt a sense of belonging and connection that she had never experienced before. She knew that her family's roots run deep, and that she was just one branch on a tree that had been growing for generations.

> ## Read the story and fill in the blank spaces with the appropriate words.

The family tree

- As soon as _____ heard that her social studies project was on creating a family tree, she couldn't wait to get started.
- She loved learning about history and discovering more about her _____, and this was the perfect opportunity to do just that.
- Emma began by interviewing her _____ and _____ about their ancestors.
- Her parents told her about their great-grandparents who had emigrated from _____ to start a new life in America.
- Her grandparents shared stories of their own childhoods and the hardships they faced during the Great _____.
- Emma's curiosity grew with each conversation, and she delved deeper into her _____.
- She searched online for public _____ and scanned old photo albums, piecing together her family tree one branch at a time.
- As she worked on her project, Emma discovered fascinating stories about her ancestors, stories of bravery, resilience, and determination. She learned that her great-great-grandfather had fought in _____, that her great-grandmother had been a suffragette, and that her grandfather had served in the Korean War.
- Emma was amazed at how much she had discovered through this _____.
- She felt like a _____, uncovering secrets, and solving mysteries. But what she enjoyed most were the connections she made between the people on her family tree.

Read the story and circle whether the statement is true or false. If the statement is false, provide the correct answer for it.

mma's social studies project was about creating a family tree.

True   False

_____
_____

mma wasn't interested in history or learning more about her roots.

True   False

_____
_____
_____

Emma discovered stories of bravery, resilience, and determination about her ancestors.

True   False

_____
_____
_____

Emma's teacher was not impressed by her project.

True   False

_____
_____

Emma felt a sense of disconnection from her family after completing the project.

True   False

_____
_____
_____

What was Emma's social studies project about?

What kind of stories did Emma discover about her ancestors?

How did Emma piece together her family tree?

Was Emma proud of the diversity in her family?

How did Emma feel after completing the project?

As soon as Emma heard that her social studies project was on creating a family tree, she couldn't wait to get started.	22
She loved learning about history and discovering more about her roots, and this was the perfect opportunity to do just that.	43
Emma began by interviewing her parents and grandparents about their ancestors.	54
Her parents told her about their great-grandparents who had emigrated from Europe to start a new life in America.	73
Her grandparents shared stories of their own childhoods and the hardships they faced during the Great Depression.	90
Emma's curiosity grew with each conversation, and she delved deeper into her past.	103
She searched online for public records and scanned old photo albums, piecing together her family tree one branch at a time.	124
As she worked on her project, Emma discovered fascinating stories about her ancestors - stories of bravery, resilience, and determination.	144
She learned that her great-great-grandfather had fought in World War I, that her great-grandmother had been a suffragette, and that her grandfather had served in the Korean War.	172
Emma was amazed at how much she had discovered through this project.	184
She felt like a detective, uncovering secrets, and solving mysteries.	194
But what she enjoyed most were the connections she made between the people on her family tree.	211
She realized that her family was a patchwork quilt of different cultures, traditions, and experiences.	226

She felt proud of the diversity in her family and the different paths that her relatives had taken. Emma knew that these stories would continue to be passed down and woven into the fabric of her family's identity.	264
When Emma presented her family tree to her class, her teacher was impressed by the amount of detail and effort she had put into the project.	290
Emma was proud to share her findings with her classmates, and even more proud to share the stories of her ancestors.	311
The project had given Emma a new appreciation for her family and where she came from.	341
She knew that she would continue to explore her family's history and learn more about the people who had come before her.	349
As she looked at the completed family tree, Emma felt a sense of belonging and connection that she had never experienced before.	371
She knew that her family's roots run deep, and that she was just one branch on a tree that had been growing for generations.	395

Date			
Words per minute			
Number of errors			

Family

_____
- -
_____

Tree

_____
- -
_____

Ancestors

_____
- -
_____

Generations

_____
- -
_____

Old

_____
- -
_____

Photos

_____
- -
_____

Make a story using only five
verbs from the following.

heard   creating   discovering
searched   fought   uncovering
solving   share

In a quaint town, young Oliver uncovers his family's captivating tale through an old photograph album. The album reveals a lineage of courageous pioneers and charismatic ancestors who left their mark on history. Oliver's great-grandfather was a charming gentleman, while his great-grandmother embodied grace and kindness. Each generation displayed resilience, generosity, and industriousness, forming a strong family tree deeply rooted in love. Inspired by their extraordinary heritage, Oliver embraces his sense of belonging and vows to carry their virtues forward. With a newfound purpose, he sets out to create his own chapter in the remarkable tapestry of their family's journey.

Story

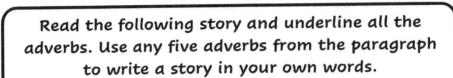

Read the following story and underline all the adverbs. Use any five adverbs from the paragraph to write a story in your own words.

In a bustling city, young Ethan eagerly delves into his family's mysterious past. Through an aged family tree chart, he discovers hidden secrets and embarks on a thrilling genealogical adventure. Carefully, he unravels the tangled branches, tracing his ancestors' footsteps across time. Courageously, Ethan uncovers his great-grandfather's daring exploits, and compassionately unearths his great-grandmother's selflessly hidden acts of kindness. Patiently, he unearths forgotten stories, diligently piecing together a rich tapestry of his heritage. With newfound understanding, Ethan gratefully embraces his roots, cherishing the tenacity, resilience, and passion that define his family tree. Inspired, he ventures forth, determined to honor their legacy and create a brighter future.

Story

Find and circle the words written below.

family   tree   ancestors
adventure   grandfather
grandmother

b	f	a	m	i	l	y	l	t	h	y	e
e	s	w	i	m	k	k	q	j	l	m	r
s	t	h	o	i	m	p	a	n	z	e	u
s	e	p	i	g	p	e	p	v	e	m	t
g	r	a	n	d	f	a	t	h	e	r	n
l	n	r	p	a	n	e	g	e	e	c	e
i	a	l	e	e	p	i	q	e	e	z	v
m	l	s	j	l	u	j	n	c	r	b	d
a	n	c	e	s	t	o	r	s	t	w	a
f	g	r	a	n	d	m	o	t	h	e	r

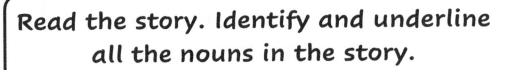

Animal Habitats

You have probably learned about different types of animals and their characteristics. One thing that is important to understand about animals is their habitat - the place where they live.

Just like humans, animals need a place to call home. However, unlike humans who can build their own homes, animals rely on nature to provide them with their habitat. Let's explore some of the different animal habitats that you may have heard about.

Forests are a common habitat for many animals. They provide a lot of shelter and food for a variety of creatures like deer, squirrels, birds, and bears. The trees in a forest provide shelter from the sun and rain, and the leaves and branches provide food and hiding places for many animals.

The desert is another type of habitat. They are hot and dry, which makes them a challenging place to live. But some animals, like camels, snakes, scorpions, and lizards, have adapted to the desert's conditions and can survive there. These animals have special features that help them conserve water, like long noses or bodies that don't lose moisture easily.

Another type of habitat is the ocean. The ocean is home to a diverse range of animals like fish, whales, dolphins, and sharks. Some animals, like sea turtles, spend most of their time in the water but come to land to lay their eggs. The ocean is also a source of food for many animals.

Grasslands are another important animal habitat. They are vast expanses of land covered in grass and few trees. Animals like zebras, giraffes, lions, and hyenas call this habitat home. Grasslands provide a lot of food for grazing animals, as well as predators who hunt those grazers.

Finally, we have wetlands. These are areas where water is present most of the year. Animals like alligators, frogs, ducks, and beavers thrive in this habitat. Wetlands are essential for filtering water and preventing floods, making them an important part of the ecosystem.

As you can see, there are many different types of animal habitats, each with its own unique features and characteristics. Understanding these habitats is important for learning about the animals that live in them and the roles they play in our environment.

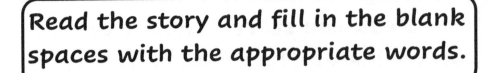

Animal Habitats

- You have probably learned about different types of _____ and their characteristics.
- One thing that is important to understand about animals is their _____ - the place where they live.
- Just like humans, animals need a place to call _____.
- However, unlike humans who can build their own homes, animals rely on _____ to provide them with their habitat.
- Let's explore some of the _____ animal habitats that you may have heard about.
- _____ are a common habitat for many animals.
- They provide a lot of shelter and _____ for a variety of creatures like deer, squirrels, birds, and bears.
- The _____ in a forest provide shelter from the sun and rain, and the leaves and branches provide food and hiding places for many animals.
- _____ are another type of habitat.
- They are _____ and _____, which makes them a challenging place to live.
- But some animals, like _____, snakes, scorpions, and lizards, have adapted to the desert's conditions and can survive there.
- These animals have special features that help them conserve _____, like long noses or bodies that don't lose moisture easily.
- Another type of habitat is the _____.
- The ocean is home to a diverse range of animals like fish, _____, _____, and sharks. Some animals, like sea turtles, spend most of their time in the water but come to land to lay their eggs.

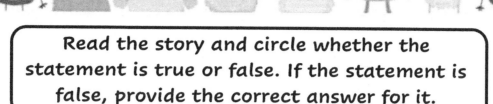

Animals do not need a place to call home.

True   False

The ocean is not home to many animals.

True   False

The desert is an easy habitat for animals to live in.

True   False

Wetlands are important for filtering water and preventing floods.

True   False

Wetlands are important for filtering water and preventing floods.

True   False

Forests provide shelter and food for a variety of animals.

True   False

Grasslands do not provide food for grazing animals.

True   False

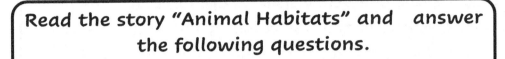

What is an animal habitat?

_____

_____

_____

_____

What are some common forest animals?

_____

_____

_____

_____

What special features do desert animals have that help them survive in their habitat?

_____

_____

_____

_____

_____

_____

_____

Why are wetlands important for the ecosystem?

_____

_____

_____

_____

_____

_____

What kinds of animals live in grasslands?

_____

_____

_____

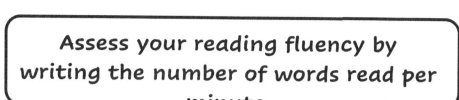

You have probably learned about different types of animals and their characteristics.	12
One thing that is important to understand about animals is their habitat - the place where they live.	30
Just like humans, animals need a place to call home. However, unlike humans who can build their own homes, animals rely on nature to provide them with their habitat.	59
Let's explore some of the different animal habitats that you may have heard about.	73
Forests are a common habitat for many animals.	81
They provide a lot of shelter and food for a variety of creatures like deer, squirrels, birds, and bears.	100
The trees in a forest provide shelter from the sun and rain, and the leaves and branches provide food and hiding places for many animals.	125
The desert is another type of habitat.	131
They are hot and dry, which makes them a challenging place to live.	144
But some animals, like camels, snakes, scorpions, and lizards, have adapted to the desert's conditions and can survive there.	163
These animals have special features that help them conserve water, like long noses or bodies that don't lose moisture easily.	183
Another type of habitat is the ocean.	193
The ocean is home to a diverse range of animals like fish, whales, dolphins, and sharks. Some animals, like sea turtles, spend most of their time in the water but come to land to lay their eggs	227
The ocean is also a source of food for many animals.	238
Grasslands are another important animal habitat.	245
They are vast expanses of land covered in grass and few trees.	256

Animals like zebras, giraffes, lions, and hyenas call this habitat home. Grasslands provide a lot of food for grazing animals, as well as predators who hunt those grazers.	284
Finally, we have wetlands.	288
These are areas where water is present most of the year. Animals like alligators, frogs, ducks, and beavers thrive in this habitat.	311
Wetlands are essential for filtering water and preventing floods, making them an important part of the ecosystem.	327
As you can see, there are many different types of animal habitats, each with its own unique features and characteristics.	348
Understanding these habitats is important for learning about the animals that live in them and the roles they play in our environment.	369

Date			
Words per minute			
Number of errors			

Make sentences using the words written below.

Habitat

_____
- -
_____

Animals

_____
- -
_____

Home

_____
- -
_____

Forests

_____
- -
_____

Deserts

_____
- -
_____

Ocean

_____
- -
_____

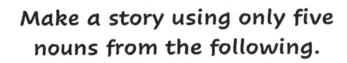

Nature   Forests   shelter   Food
Creatures   Deer   Squirrels   Bird
Bears   Trees   Leaves   Branches
Deserts   Camels   Snakes

_____
_____
_____
_____
_____
_____
_____
_____
_____
_____
_____
_____
_____
_____
_____
_____
_____
_____

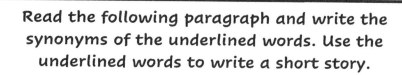

Animal habitats are the <u>places</u> where different animals live and thrive. These habitats can be found all over the world, from forests to deserts to oceans. Understanding animal habitats is <u>important</u> because it helps us <u>learn</u> about the different types of animals that exist and how they <u>survive</u> in their environments. Each habitat has its own <u>unique</u> features that provide shelter, food, and a sense of safety for the animals that call it home. By protecting these habitats, we can help preserve the natural world and ensure that these amazing creatures continue to thrive for generations to come.

Words	places	important	learn	survive	unique
Synonyms					

Story

_____
_____
_____
_____
_____
_____
_____
_____
_____
_____
_____
_____
_____
_____
_____
_____
_____
_____
_____

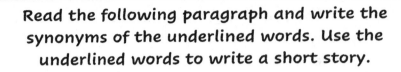

The ocean is a <u>vast</u> and fascinating habitat that is home to a diverse array of creatures. It covers over 70% of the Earth's surface and is filled with a variety of plant and animal life. The ocean is an <u>ever-changing</u> environment that can be both <u>peaceful</u> and powerful. Some of the creatures that call the ocean home include whales, dolphins, sharks, and fish. While the ocean can be <u>serene</u> and calm at times, it can also be tumultuous and dangerous during storms or rough weather. The ocean is often associated with tranquility, but it can also be turbulent, placid, shallow, deep, and <u>clear</u> or murky, making it a truly unique and complex habitat.

Words	vast	ever-changing	peaceful	serene	clear
Antonyms					

Story

_____
_____
_____
_____
_____
_____
_____
_____
_____
_____
_____
_____
_____
_____
_____
_____
_____
_____

Find and circle the words written below.

animals   habitats   ocean
deserts   forests   wetlands
snakes   bears   camels

m	a	r	i	a	a	l	s	f	w	h	p
p	s	o	s	c	k	k	q	i	s	e	e
s	n	t	h	i	m	p	a	n	t	e	s
r	u	h	k	g	p	e	p	g	s	m	t
a	c	a	m	e	l	s	j	e	e	n	a
e	r	u	i	t	s	e	g	r	r	a	t
b	r	s	e	k	a	n	s	s	o	e	i
w	e	t	l	a	n	d	s	c	f	c	b
m	i	p	s	t	r	e	s	e	d	o	a
a	n	i	m	a	l	s	k	e	y	t	h

Camping adventures

It was a long weekend, and my friends and I decided to go camping in the nearby forest. We had been planning this trip for weeks and were excited to finally set off on our adventure. We packed our backpacks with all the essentials, including tents, sleeping bags, cooking supplies, and plenty of food and water.

As we hiked through the forest, we marveled at the beauty of nature around us. The sun was shining, and the birds were chirping as we made our way deeper into the woods. We found a clearing near a small stream and decided to set up camp there.

We quickly got to work setting up our tents and gathering firewood for a campfire later that night. After our campsite was set up, we decided to go explore the surrounding area. We hiked along the stream, admiring the tall trees and the rushing water.

As the sun began to set, we returned to our campsite and started a fire. We roasted hot dogs and marshmallows over the flames, telling stories and laughing together. As the night wore on, we settled into our tents for the night, listening to the sounds of the forest around us.

In the middle of the night, I was awoken by a loud rustling sound outside my tent. I cautiously unzipped the door and peered out into the darkness. Suddenly, a pair of glowing eyes stared back at me! I quickly zipped the tent flap shut and woke up my friends.

We listened quietly as the animal outside rummaged through our food supplies. It was a raccoon! We had forgotten to put our food away properly, and now we were paying the price. After the raccoon finished

rummaging through our supplies, it scampered off into the woods. We all laughed nervously about the close encounter and made a mental note to be more careful with our food.

The next day, we decided to go on a longer hike through the forest. We followed a trail that led us up a steep hill and through a dense thicket. As we reached the top, we were rewarded with a stunning view of the valley below. We sat down on a nearby outcropping to take it all in.

After our hike, we returned to our campsite and spent the rest of the day lounging by the stream and playing games. That night, we gathered around the campfire once again, enjoying each other's company and the warmth of the flames.

As we packed up our campsite on the final day, I felt a sense of sadness that our adventure was coming to an end. We had experienced so much together in such a short amount of time. But I knew that we would always cherish the memories of our camping adventure in the woods.

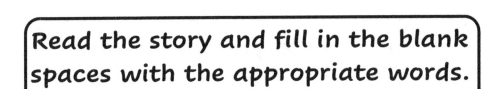

Camping adventures

- It was a long weekend, and my friends and I decided to go _____ in the nearby forest.
- We had been planning this trip for weeks and were excited to finally set off on our _____.
- We packed our backpacks with all the essentials, including - _____, sleeping _____, cooking supplies, and plenty of food and water.
- As we hiked through the forest, we marveled at the beauty of _____ around us.
- The sun was shining, and the birds were _____ as we made our way deeper into the woods.
- We found a clearing near a small _____ and decided to set up camp there.
- We quickly got to work setting up our tents and gathering _____ for a campfire later that night.
- After our campsite was set up, we decided to go explore the _____ area.
- We hiked along the _____, admiring the tall trees and the rushing water.
- As the sun began to set, we returned to our campsite and started a _____.
- We roasted _____ and marshmallows over the flames, telling stories and laughing together.
- As the night wore on, we settled into our tents for the night, listening to the _____ of the forest around us.
- In the middle of the night, I was awoken by a loud _____ sound outside my tent.

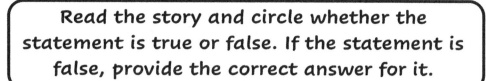

Read the story and circle whether the
statement is true or false. If the statement is
false, provide the correct answer for it.

The group packed all the essentials for their camping trip.

True   False

They set up camp near a lake.

True   False

The group explored the surrounding forest.

True   False

They saw a raccoon outside their tent at night.

True   False

The group had properly stored their food.

True   False

They went on a long hike through the forest.

True   False

The group felt sad when they had to leave and return home.

True   False

What did the group pack for their camping trip?

Where did they decide to set up camp?

What did the group see when they hiked to the top of a hill?

What did they do when they encountered a raccoon at night?

How did the group feel when it was time to leave and return home??

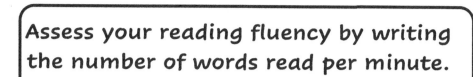

It was a long weekend, and my friends and I decided to go camping in the nearby forest.	18
We had been planning this trip for weeks and were excited to finally set off on our adventure.	36
We packed our backpacks with all the essentials, including tents, sleeping bags, cooking supplies, and plenty of food and water.	56
As we hiked through the forest, we marveled at the beauty of nature around us.	71
The sun was shining, and the birds were chirping as we made our way deeper into the woods.	89
We found a clearing near a small stream and decided to set up camp here.	106
We quickly got to work setting up our tents and gathering firewood for a campfire later that night.	122
After our campsite was set up, we decided to go explore the surrounding area.	136
We hiked along the stream, admiring the tall trees and the rushing water.	149
As the sun began to set, we returned to our campsite and started a fire.	164
We roasted hot dogs and marshmallows over the flames, telling stories and laughing together.	178
As the night wore on, we settled into our tents for the night, listening to the sounds of the forest around us.	200
In the middle of the night, I was awoken by a loud rustling sound outside my tent.	217
I cautiously unzipped the door and peered out into the darkness.	228
Suddenly, a pair of glowing eyes stared back at me! I quickly zipped the tent flap shut and woke up my friends.	250

We listened quietly as the animal outside rummaged through our food supplies.	263
It was a raccoon! We had forgotten to put our food away properly, and now we were paying the price.	282
After the raccoon finished rummaging through our supplies, it scampered off into the woods.	306
We all laughed nervously about the close encounter and made a mental note to be more careful with our food.	325
The next day, we decided to go on a longer hike through the forest.	340
We followed a trail that led us up a steep hill and through a dense thicket.	355
As we reached the top, we were rewarded with a stunning view of the valley below.	372
We sat down on a nearby outcropping to take it all in.	383
After our hike, we returned to our campsite and spent the rest of the day lounging by the stream and playing games.	405
That night, we gathered around the campfire once again, enjoying each other's company and the warmth of the flames.	424
As we packed up our campsite on the final day, I felt a sense of sadness that our adventure was coming to an end.	448
We had experienced so much together in such a short amount of time. But I knew that we would always cherish the memories of our camping adventure in the woods.	478

Date			
Words per minute			
Number of errors			

Make sentences using the words written below.

Camping

_____

_____

Adventure

_____

_____

Forest

_____

_____

Backpacks

_____

_____

Nature

_____

_____

Raccoon

_____

_____

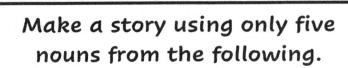

Make a story using only five nouns from the following.

Friends   Camping   Forest
Backpacks   Tents   Sleeping bags
Supplies   Food   Water   Sun   Birds

_____
- -
_____

_____
- -
_____

_____
- -
_____

_____
- -
_____

_____
- -
_____

_____
- -
_____

> ### Read the following paragraph, identify, and underline all the adjectives. Use the underlined words to write a short story.

Last summer, my family and I went on a camping trip to a remote forest in the mountains. The air was crisp and cool as we drove up the winding road, surrounded by tall trees and soaring peaks. When we arrived at our campsite, we were greeted by a peaceful and serene setting. Our tents were set up on a soft bed of pine needles, with a babbling brook nearby. The surrounding woods were dark and mysterious, but also inviting and comforting. We spent our days hiking along rugged trails, breathing in the fresh mountain air, and exploring the hidden wonders of the forest. At night, we gathered around the campfire, roasting marshmallows and telling stories under a star-filled sky. It was a magical and unforgettable experience, one filled with adventure, beauty, and relaxation.

Story

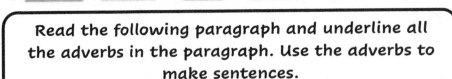

Camping adventures can be exhilaratingly fun and excitingly adventurous, especially when you explore the great outdoors with friends or family. As we hiked through the dense forest, we breathed deeply, feeling the fresh mountain air invigoratingly fill our lungs. We trekked on the winding trails, eagerly discovering new paths and secret spots of the wilderness. The sun shone brilliantly, casting dappled light across our path, illuminating the verdant trees and lush undergrowth. The stream flowed gently, soothingly bubbling over rocks, providing a calming melody for our journey. We set up camp efficiently, quickly pitching our tents and making a fire skillfully. The stars shone radiantly in the clear sky, brilliantly twinkling above us as we sat cozily around the campfire, telling stories animatedly and laughing heartily. It was an experience remarkably worth living, and we couldn't wait to do it again.

Adverbs	Sentences

Find and circle the words written below.

camping   adventure   hike
sun   exciting   sleeping
forest   tents   firewood

f	i	r	e	w	o	o	d	f	w	a	c
s	h	i	k	e	k	s	u	n	f	e	e
l	n	c	s	i	m	b	p	i	r	x	r
e	e	h	t	g	p	e	g	l	u	c	u
e	d	l	a	k	r	c	j	l	i	i	t
p	i	r	r	a	b	e	g	e	t	t	n
i	t	e	n	t	s	s	q	h	s	i	e
n	f	o	r	e	s	t	i	s	n	n	v
g	p	y	o	a	m	y	d	s	s	g	d
c	a	m	p	i	n	g	l	i	s	m	a

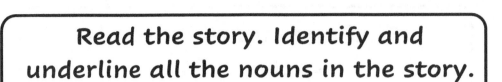

Healthy picnic

The sun was shining, the birds were chirping, and the breeze was just right as the Johnson family packed up their car and set out for a fun-filled picnic adventure. But this wasn't just any picnic; it was going to be a day filled with healthy eating and wholesome snacks.

As they drove to the park, the family chatted excitedly about the delicious and nutritious food they had packed for the day. There were fresh fruits like strawberries, blueberries, and grapes, as well as crisp veggies like carrots, celery, and bell peppers. They also brought along homemade hummus and guacamole for dipping, along with whole-grain crackers and pita bread.

When they arrived at the park, the family found a cozy spot under a large oak tree, spreading out their blanket and arranging their healthy treats on a large platter. The kids eagerly grabbed handfuls of grapes and berries, while mom and dad dug into the hummus and veggies.

As they ate and laughed and enjoyed the beautiful day, the Johnsons talked about the importance of healthy eating and how it can benefit the whole family. They discussed how eating a balanced diet can help prevent chronic diseases like heart disease and diabetes, and how it can give them more energy and help them feel better overall.

After finishing their picnic, the family went for a walk around the park, taking in the beautiful scenery and enjoying some physical activity. They kicked around a soccer ball and played a game of Frisbee, feeling invigorated and energized from their healthy snacks and exercise.

As the day ended, the Johnsons packed up their things and headed back home, feeling proud of themselves for choosing to have a healthy and fun-filled picnic. They made a promise to each other to continue making healthy choices and living an active lifestyle, knowing that it would lead to a happier and healthier life for them all.

In conclusion, healthy eating is not only good for the body, but also for the mind and soul. The Johnson family's picnic adventure shows that healthy food can be delicious and fun, and that it can bring families together in a meaningful way. By making small changes to their diet and lifestyle, they are setting themselves up for a lifetime of health and happiness.

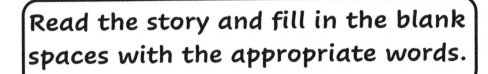

Healthy picnic

- The sun was shining, the birds were chirping, and the breeze was just right as the _____ family packed up their car and set out for a fun-filled picnic adventure.
- But this wasn't just any picnic: it was going to be a day filled with _____ eating and wholesome snacks.
- As they drove to the park, the family chatted excitedly about the delicious and _____ food they had packed for the day.
- There were fresh fruits like strawberries, _____, and grapes, as well as crisp veggies like carrots, celery, and bell peppers.
- They also brought along homemade _____ and guacamole for dipping, along with whole-grain crackers and pita bread.
- When they arrived at the park, the family found a cozy spot under a large _____ tree, spreading out their blanket and arranging their healthy treats on a large platter.
- The kids eagerly grabbed handfuls of grapes and berries, while mom and dad dug into the hummus and _____.
- As they ate and laughed and enjoyed the beautiful day, the Johnsons talked about the _____ of healthy eating and how it can benefit the whole family.
- They discussed how eating a balanced diet can help prevent chronic diseases like _____ and diabetes, and how it can give them more energy and help them feel better overall.
- After finishing their picnic, the family went for a walk around the park, taking in the beautiful scenery and enjoying some _____.

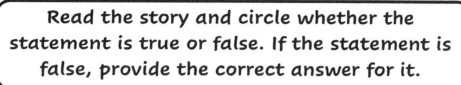

The Johnson family went on a picnic filled with unhealthy snacks.

True   False

_____

The family talked about the benefits of healthy eating during their picnic.

True   False

_____

The family didn't do any physical activity during their picnic.

True   False

_____

Healthy eating can help prevent chronic diseases like heart disease and diabetes.

True   False

_____

The Johnson family ate junk food for their picnic and felt guilty about it afterwards.

True   False

_____

The Johnson family promised to continue making healthy choices and living an active lifestyle after their picnic.

True   False

_____

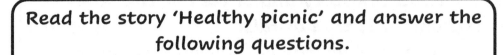

Read the story 'Healthy picnic' and answer the following questions.

What did the Johnson family pack for their picnic?

_____

_____

What kinds of fruits and veggies did the Johnsons bring for their picnic?

_____

_____

_____

Why did the family discuss the benefits of healthy eating during their picnic?

_____

_____

_____

_____

_____

What kinds of physical activities did the Johnson family do during their picnic?

_____

_____

_____

What promise did the Johnson family make to each other after their picnic?

_____

_____

_____

_____

The sun was shining, the birds were chirping, and the breeze was just right as the Johnson family packed up their car and set out for a fun-filled picnic adventure.	30
But this wasn't just any picnic: it was going to be a day filled with healthy eating and wholesome snacks.	50
As they drove to the park, the family chatted excitedly about the delicious and nutritious food they had packed for the day.	73
There were fresh fruits like strawberries, blueberries, and grapes, as well as crisp veggies like carrots, celery, and bell peppers.	92
They also brought along homemade hummus and guacamole for dipping, along with whole-grain crackers and pita bread.	109
When they arrived at the park, the family found a cozy spot under a large oak tree, spreading out their blanket and arranging their healthy treats on a large platter.	140
The kids eagerly grabbed handfuls of grapes and berries, while mom and dad dug into the hummus and veggies.	158
From eating breakfast together to playtime in the fields, Mary and Molly were always by each other's side.	143
As they ate and laughed and enjoyed the beautiful day, the Johnsons talked about the importance of healthy eating and how it can benefit the whole family.	185
They discussed how eating a balanced diet can help prevent chronic diseases like heart disease and diabetes, and how it can give them more energy and help them feel better overall.	216
After finishing their picnic, the family went for a walk around the park, taking in the beautiful scenery and enjoying some physical activity.	239
They kicked around a soccer ball and played a game of Frisbee, feeling invigorated and energized from their healthy snacks and exercise.	261

As the day ended, the Johnsons packed up their things and headed back home, feeling proud of themselves for choosing to have a healthy and fun-filled picnic.	289
They made a promise to each other to continue making healthy choices and living an active lifestyle, knowing that it would lead to a happier and healthier life for them all.	319
In conclusion, healthy eating is not only good for the body, but also for the mind and soul.	337
The Johnson family's picnic adventure shows that healthy food can be delicious and fun, and that it can bring families together in a meaningful way.	362
By making small changes to their diet and lifestyle, they are setting themselves up for a lifetime of health and happiness.	383

Date			
Words per minute			
Number of errors			

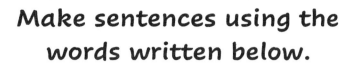

Make sentences using the words written below.

Nutritious

_____
- -
_____

Food

_____
- -
_____

Healthy

_____
- -
_____

Picnic

_____
- -
_____

Family

_____
- -
_____

Diet

_____
- -
_____

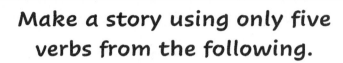

Make a story using only five
verbs from the following.

sun   birds   breeze   car   picnic
food   fruits   strawberries
blueberries   grapes   veggies
carrots   celery   bell peppers

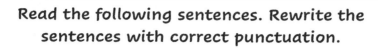

1. healthy eating is important for maintaining a balanced diet and preventing chronic diseases like heart disease and diabetes

_____

_____

2. eating plenty of fruits and vegetables can help you get the vitamins minerals and fiber your body needs to stay healthy

_____

_____

3. whole grain foods like brown rice quinoa and whole wheat bread are good sources of complex carbohydrates that provide sustained energy

_____

_____

4. eating lean proteins like chicken fish and legumes can help build and repair muscles and keep you feeling full and satisfied

_____

_____

5. snacking on nuts seeds and dried fruit can be a healthy way to satisfy your hunger between meals

_____

6. drinking plenty of water throughout the day can help keep your body hydrated and flush out toxins

_____

7. choosing healthy fats like avocado nuts and olive oil can provide essential fatty acids and promote heart health

_____

_____

Healthy eating is an important part of maintaining a healthy lifestyle. By focusing on incorporating nutrient-dense foods into your diet, you can give your body the fuel it needs to function at its best. Some key foods to include in a healthy diet include fruits, vegetables, whole grains, lean proteins, and healthy fats. Additionally, it's important to drink plenty of water and limit your intake of processed and sugary foods. By making small changes to your diet and lifestyle, you can improve your overall health and well-being. So why not start today? Your body will thank you for it.

Nouns	Pronouns	Sentences

Find and circle the words written below.

healthy   eating   picnic
nutrition   food   fruits
vegetable   water

h	e	a	t	i	n	g	e	d	w	n	p
e	c	l	i	m	b	a	c	a	e	u	i
a	n	a	n	i	m	a	l	s	l	t	c
l	e	y	t	g	p	e	g	e	b	r	n
t	s	n	n	y	r	c	j	a	a	i	i
h	t	e	r	t	e	e	g	l	t	c	c
y	i	g	s	s	t	s	y	t	e	i	r
a	u	t	e	i	a	s	r	h	g	o	l
h	r	k	r	m	w	i	a	y	e	n	p
f	f	o	o	d	m	p	m	j	v	c	z

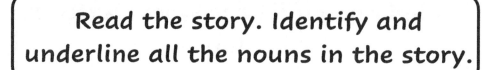

The mighty Amazon River

The Amazon River is one of the most awe-inspiring and majestic waterways in the world. It stretches over 4,000 miles and flows through nine different countries, including Brazil, Peru, and Colombia. Known for its diverse ecosystem and abundant wildlife, the Amazon River is a vital source of life and livelihood for millions of people who call the surrounding region home.

At its widest point, the Amazon River can be over 24 miles across, with depths reaching up to 300 feet. That's wider and deeper than many of the world's other great rivers, including the Nile and the Mississippi. And while the Amazon doesn't have quite as much water flow as the latter two rivers, it still pours an incredible 7 million cubic feet of water into the Atlantic Ocean every second.

One of the most fascinating things about the Amazon River is its rich biodiversity. Thousands of different species of plants and animals can be found along its banks, including jaguars, anacondas, pink dolphins, and giant otters. In fact, it's estimated that the Amazon Basin is home to more than 16,000 different species of trees alone.

Of course, the Amazon River isn't just a natural wonder - it's also an essential resource for the people who live along its banks. Indigenous communities have relied on the river for centuries for transportation, food, and water. In recent years, the Amazon has become increasingly important for industries like logging, mining, and agriculture, which can have both positive and negative impacts on the health of the river and its surrounding ecosystem.

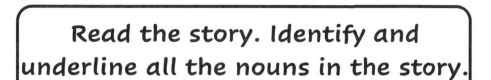

Read the story. Identify and underline all the nouns in the story.

Despite its importance, the Amazon River also faces significant threats from climate change, habitat loss, and pollution. Deforestation, in particular, has been a major issue in recent years, with vast swaths of rainforest being cleared for cattle grazing and soybean production. This destruction not only harms the millions of species that call the Amazon home but also contributes to climate change by releasing large amounts of carbon dioxide into the atmosphere.

Despite these challenges, there is hope for the future of the Amazon River. Conservation efforts are underway to protect the river and its surrounding ecosystem, and many local communities are working to find sustainable ways to use its resources without damaging the environment. With continued effort and dedication, we can help ensure that the mighty Amazon River remains a vital source of life and wonder for generations to come.

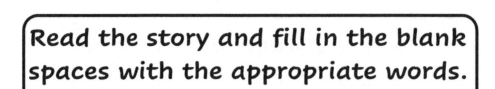

The mighty Amazon River

- The Amazon River is one of the most awe-inspiring and majestic _____ in the world.
- It stretches over _____ miles and flows through nine different countries, including Brazil, Peru, and Colombia.
- Known for its diverse _____ and abundant wildlife, the Amazon River is a vital source of life and livelihood for millions of people who call the surrounding region home.
- At its widest point, the Amazon River can be over _____ across, with depths reaching up to 300 feet.
- That's wider and deeper than many of the world's other great rivers, including the _____ and the Mississippi.
- And while the Amazon doesn't have quite as much water flow as the latter two rivers, it still pours an incredible _____ cubic feet of water into the Atlantic Ocean every second.
- One of the most fascinating things about the Amazon River is its rich _____.
- Thousands of different species of plants and animals can be found along its banks, including _____, _____, _____, and giant otters.
- In fact, it's estimated that the Amazon Basin is home to more than _____ different species of trees alone.
- Of course, the Amazon River isn't just a _____ wonder - it's also an essential resource for the people who live along its banks.
- Indigenous communities have relied on the river for centuries for transportation, food, and _____.

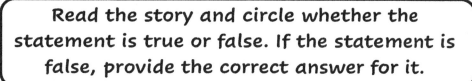

The Amazon River is over 4,000 miles long.

True   False

_____

The Amazon River flows through ten different countries.

True   False

_____

The Amazon River can be up to 24 miles wide at its widest point.

True   False

_____

The Amazon River has less water flow than the Nile and Mississippi rivers.

True   False

_____

Indigenous communities have never relied on the Amazon River for transportation, food, or water.

True   False

_____
_____

Deforestation is a major threat to the health of the Amazon River and its surrounding ecosystem.

True   False

_____
_____
_____

What countries does the Amazon River flow through?

What types of plants and animals can be found along the Amazon River?

How wide and deep can the Amazon River get?

What are some of the threats to the health of the Amazon River?

What are some conservation efforts underway to protect the Amazon River and its surrounding ecosystem?

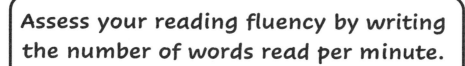

The Amazon River is one of the most awe-inspiring and majestic waterways in the world.	15
It stretches over 4,000 miles and flows through nine different countries, including Brazil, Peru, and Colombia.	31
Known for its diverse ecosystem and abundant wildlife, the Amazon River is a vital source of life and livelihood for millions of people who call the surrounding region home.	60
At its widest point, the Amazon River can be over 24 miles across, with depths reaching up to 300 feet.	80
That's wider and deeper than many of the world's other great rivers, including the Nile and the Mississippi.	98
And while the Amazon doesn't have quite as much water flow as the latter two rivers, it still pours an incredible 7 million cubic feet of water into the Atlantic Ocean every second.	131
One of the most fascinating things about the Amazon River is its rich biodiversity.	145
Thousands of different species of plants and animals can be found along its banks, including jaguars, anacondas, pink dolphins, and giant otters.	167
In fact, it's estimated that the Amazon Basin is home to more than 16,000 different species of trees alone.	186
Of course, the Amazon River isn't just a natural wonder - it's also an essential resource for the people who live along its banks.	210
Indigenous communities have relied on the river for centuries for transportation, food, and water.	224
In recent years, the Amazon has become increasingly important for industries like logging, mining, and agriculture, which can have both positive and negative impacts on the health of the river and its surrounding ecosystem.	258

Despite its importance, the Amazon River also faces significant threats from climate change, habitat loss, and pollution.	275
Deforestation, in particular, has been a major issue in recent years, with vast swaths of rainforest being cleared for cattle grazing and soybean production.	299
This destruction not only harms the millions of species that call the Amazon home but also contributes to climate change by releasing large amounts of carbon dioxide into the atmosphere.	329
Despite these challenges, there is hope for the future of the Amazon River.	342
Conservation efforts are underway to protect the river and its surrounding ecosystem, and many local communities are working to find sustainable ways to use its resources without damaging the environment.	372
With continued effort and dedication, we can help ensure that the mighty Amazon River remains a vital source of life and wonder for generations to come.	398

Date			
Words per minute			
Number of errors			

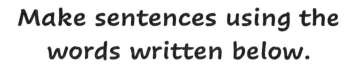

Make sentences using the words written below.

River

_____

- -

_____

Ecosystem

_____

- -

_____

Flow

_____

- -

_____

Water

_____

- -

_____

Rich

_____

- -

_____

Transportation

_____

- -

_____

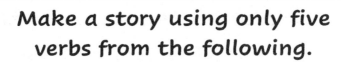

Make a story using only five verbs from the following.

stretches flows call pour found
rely cleared harms contributes
protects use damage remains

_____

_____

_____

_____

_____

_____

_____

_____

_____

_____

_____

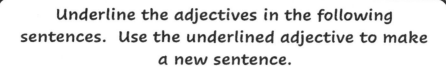

1. The breathtaking Amazon River is one of the longest and most powerful rivers in the world.

_____

2. The Amazon River boasts an incredible diversity of plants and animals, making it a truly awe-inspiring natural wonder.

_____

3. The mighty Amazon River flows through some of the most remote and untouched regions on earth.

_____

4. The Amazon River is an essential resource for the millions of people who call the surrounding region home.

_____

5. The Amazon River is a crucial habitat for countless species of unique and exotic wildlife.

_____

6. The Amazon River's lush rainforests and vibrant ecosystems are under constant threat from deforestation and climate change.

_____

7. The Amazon River's massive size and depth make it a vital source of water and transportation for communities throughout the region.

_____

8. The Amazon River's vast network of tributaries and channels create a complex and intricate system that sustains life for millions.

_____

The Amazon River is one of the most <u>fascinating</u> natural wonders on earth. Its <u>vast</u> size and incredible biodiversity make it a truly awe-inspiring sight to behold. <u>Stretching</u> over 4,000 miles and flowing through nine different countries, the Amazon River is a <u>vital</u> source of life and livelihood for millions of people who call the <u>surrounding</u> region home. From its lush rainforests to its vast network of tributaries and channels, the Amazon River sustains an incredible <u>diversity</u> of plant and animal life, including jaguars, anacondas, pink dolphins, and giant otters. However, the Amazon River is not without its challenges. Deforestation, climate change, and pollution are all major <u>threats</u> to the health of the river and its surrounding ecosystem. Despite these challenges, there is <u>hope</u> for the <u>future</u> of the Amazon River. Conservation efforts are underway to <u>protect</u> this precious resource and ensure that it remains a vital source of life and wonder for generations to come.

S.No	Synonyms	Antonyms	Sentences
1			
2			
3			
4			
5			
6			
7			
8			
9			
10			

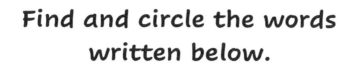

Find and circle the words written below.

Amazon   river   home
vast   channels   people
Atlantic   ocean

r	i	v	e	r	c	h	o	m	e	a	g
r	o	h	v	a	s	t	q	j	o	e	r
e	s	i	s	i	m	b	e	i	r	e	e
k	l	v	t	g	p	e	g	h	k	n	a
r	e	e	a	k	b	c	c	l	e	e	n
o	n	r	r	y	b	r	g	e	r	c	a
n	n	r	e	n	a	s	q	e	s	p	e
o	a	n	e	e	i	s	i	o	n	l	c
z	h	y	s	a	m	i	d	s	a	m	o
a	c	m	a	t	l	a	n	t	i	c	y
m	o	r	e	b	u	i	l	t	c	b	v
a	n	p	e	o	p	l	e	o	r	m	o

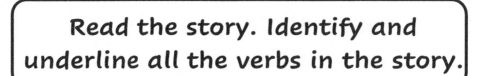

Journey to the Arctic

Rachel had always been fascinated by the Arctic, with its snow-covered landscapes and exotic wildlife. So, when she was offered the chance to embark on a journey to the Arctic, she jumped at the opportunity.

The journey began with a flight to a small town in northern Canada, where Rachel met up with her guide, a seasoned adventurer named Jack. From there, they boarded a small plane that would take them deep into the heart of the Arctic.

As they flew over the frozen tundra, Rachel's excitement grew. She was about to embark on an adventure that few people ever get to experience.

When they finally landed, Rachel and Jack set up camp near the coast, surrounded by nothing but snow and ice as far as the eye could see. The temperature was well below freezing, but Rachel was undeterred. She donned her warmest clothing and set out to explore the Arctic landscape.

As she walked through the snow, Rachel marveled at the stunning beauty of the area. The vast expanse of snow, the towering ice formations, and the occasional glimpse of a polar bear in the distance all combined to create a sense of awe and wonder that Rachel would never forget.

Over the course of the next several days, Rachel and Jack explored the Arctic, encountering all kinds of fascinating wildlife along the way. They saw herds of caribou grazing peacefully in the snow, watched as a family of arctic foxes played in the distance, and caught a glimpse of a massive walrus lounging on the ice.

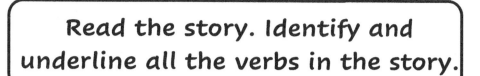

But perhaps the most impressive encounter came when they stumbled upon a group of polar bears. At first, Rachel was terrified; after all, these were some of the most fearsome predators on the planet. But as she watched from a safe distance, she couldn't help but be struck by the beauty and majesty of these magnificent creatures.

As the journey came to an end and Rachel made her way back to civilization, she knew that she had experienced something truly special. The Arctic had captured her heart in a way that she never thought possible, and she was already planning her next adventure back to this incredible part of the world.

.

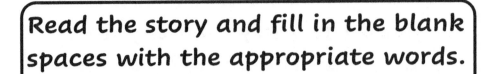

Journey to the Arctic

- Rachel had always been fascinated by the _____ with its snow-covered landscapes and exotic wildlife.
- So, when she was offered the chance to embark on a _____ to the Arctic, she jumped at the opportunity.
- The journey began with a flight to a small town in northern _____, where Rachel met up with her guide, a seasoned adventurer named Jack.
- From there, they boarded a small _____ that would take them deep into the heart of the Arctic.
- As they flew over the frozen _____, Rachel's excitement grew.
- She was about to embark on an _____ that few people ever get to experience.
- When they finally landed, Rachel and Jack set up _____ near the coast, surrounded by nothing but snow and ice as far as the eye could see.
- The temperature was well below _____, but Rachel was undeterred.
- She donned her warmest _____ and set out to explore the Arctic landscape.
- As she walked through the _____, Rachel marveled at the stunning beauty of the area.
- The vast expanse of snow, the towering ice formations, and the occasional glimpse of a _____ in the distance all combined to create a sense of awe and wonder that Rachel would never forget.

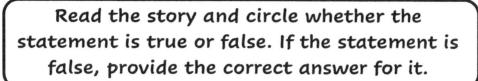

Rachel was always fascinated by the Arctic.

True   False

_____

Rachel's guide was named John.

True   False

_____

Rachel and Jack set up camp near the Equator.

True   False

_____

The temperature was well below freezing in the Arctic.

True   False

_____

Rachel and Jack encountered herds of zebras in the snow.

True   False

_____

Rachel saw a family of arctic foxes playing in the distance.

True   False

_____

The polar bears were not dangerous and Rachel was not afraid of them.

True   False

_____

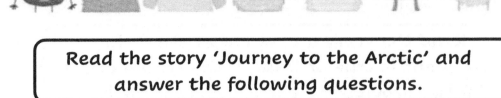

What inspired Rachel to embark on a journey to the Arctic?

_____

_____

_____

_____

Who was Rachel's guide on her journey to the Arctic?

_____

_____

_____

_____

What kind of wildlife did Rachel and Jack encounter during their exploration of the Arctic?

_____

_____

_____

_____

_____

_____

How did Rachel feel when she first saw the polar bears in the distance?

_____

_____

_____

_____

_____

What impact did the journey to the Arctic have on Rachel?

_____

_____

_____

_____

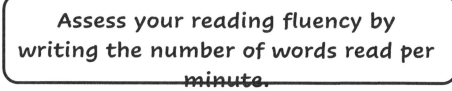

Rachel had always been fascinated by the Arctic, with its snow-covered landscapes and exotic wildlife.	15
So, when she was offered the chance to embark on a journey to the Arctic, she jumped at the opportunity.	35
The journey began with a flight to a small town in northern Canada, where Rachel met up with her guide, a seasoned adventurer named Jack.	60
From there, they boarded a small plane that would take them deep into the heart of the Arctic.	78
As they flew over the frozen tundra, Rachel's excitement grew.	89
She was about to embark on an adventure that few people ever get to experience.	103
When they finally landed, Rachel and Jack set up camp near the coast, surrounded by nothing but snow and ice as far as the eye could see.	130
The temperature was well below freezing, but Rachel was undeterred.	140
She donned her warmest clothing and set out to explore the Arctic landscape.	153
As she walked through the snow, Rachel marveled at the stunning beauty of the area.	168
The vast expanse of snow, the towering ice formations, and the occasional glimpse of a polar bear in the distance all combined to create a sense of awe and wonder that Rachel would never forget.	203
Over the course of the next several days, Rachel and Jack explored the Arctic, encountering all kinds of fascinating wildlife along the way.	227
They saw herds of caribou grazing peacefully in the snow, watched as a family of arctic foxes played in the distance, and caught a glimpse of a massive walrus lounging on the ice.	259

But perhaps the most impressive encounter came when they stumbled upon a group of polar bears.	275
At first, Rachel was terrified, after all, these were some of the most fearsome predators on the planet.	293
But as she watched from a safe distance, she couldn't help but be struck by the beauty and majesty of these magnificent creatures.	316
As the journey came to an end and Rachel made her way back to civilization, she knew that she had experienced something truly special.	341
The Arctic had captured her heart in a way that she never thought possible, and she was already planning her next adventure back to this incredible part of the world.	370

Date			
Words per minute			
Number of errors			

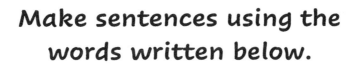

Make sentences using the words written below.

Polar

_____
- -
_____

Arctic

_____
- -
_____

Freezing

_____
- -
_____

Cold

_____
- -
_____

Ice

_____
- -
_____

Wildlife

_____
- -
_____

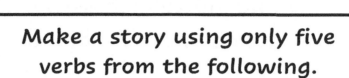

Make a story using only five verbs from the following.

embarked   jumped   landed   set up

donned   walked   marveled   saw

watched   caught   stumbled   struck

_____

- -

_____

- -

_____

_____

- -

_____

_____

- -

_____

_____

- -

_____

_____

- -

_____

> **Underline the adjectives in the following sentences. Use the underlined adjective to make a new sentence.**

1. The Arctic is a vast and desolate region that is home to many unique species of wildlife.

   _____

2. Its icy landscapes are breathtakingly beautiful, but also incredibly dangerous.

   _____

3. The Arctic's extreme temperatures make it one of the most inhospitable places on earth.

   _____

4. Despite its harsh climate, the Arctic is home to many resilient indigenous communities.

   _____

5. Climate change is having a devastating impact on the Arctic ecosystem, with melting ice and rising sea levels threatening many species of animals.

   _____

6. The Arctic's frozen expanses provide a blank canvas for exploration and discovery.

   _____

7. The Northern Lights can be seen dancing across the Arctic sky on clear winter nights, creating a truly mesmerizing spectacle.

   _____

8. The Arctic's rugged terrain requires a certain level of skill and expertise to navigate safely.

   _____

9. The Arctic's frigid waters are home to many fascinating creatures, including whales, seals, and walruses.

   _____

10. The Arctic's remote and isolated nature makes it a place of solitude and contemplation, where one can truly connect with the natural world.

    _____

Rachel had always been <u>fascinated</u> by the Arctic, with its snow-covered landscapes and <u>exotic</u> wildlife. So, when she was <u>offered</u> the chance to embark on a journey to the Arctic, she jumped at the <u>opportunity</u>. The journey began with a flight to a <u>small</u> town in northern Canada, where Rachel <u>met</u> up with her guide, a seasoned adventurer named Jack. From there, they <u>boarded</u> a small plane that would take them <u>deep</u> into the heart of the Arctic. As they flew over the <u>frozen</u> tundra, Rachel's excitement grew. She was about to <u>embark</u> on an adventure that few people ever get to experience.

S.No	Synonyms	Antonyms	Sentences
1			
2			
3			
4			
5			
6			
7			
8			
9			
10			

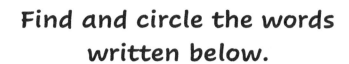

Find and circle the words written below.

Arctic   ocean   ice   freezing
Canada   small   frozen
plane   wildlife

p	s	m	a	l	l	r	o	r	o	p	c
t	b	f	r	o	z	e	n	j	o	l	n
e	e	s	i	g	n	e	d	l	l	a	o
c	e	c	t	g	u	e	g	h	k	n	i
i	w	i	l	d	l	i	f	e	p	e	a
n	i	e	r	y	o	r	g	e	r	l	d
a	t	r	e	n	p	s	q	e	s	l	a
e	p	j	a	c	x	s	i	o	n	o	n
c	f	r	e	e	z	i	n	g	s	v	a
o	a	r	c	t	i	c	t	n	r	e	c

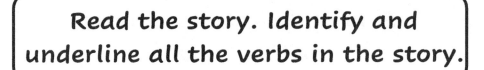

Read the story. Identify and underline all the verbs in the story.

Diving into the deep sea

Sophie had always been fascinated by the underwater world, so she decided to embark on a scuba diving adventure to explore the sea up close and personal. As she geared up in her wetsuit and tanks, she felt a thrill of excitement run through her veins. She was about to experience something truly magical.

The moment she submerged into the water, Sophie was struck by the incredible beauty of the underwater world. Schools of fish darted around her, their scales shimmering in the sunlight filtering down from above. As she swam deeper into the sea, she encountered even more incredible sights, towering coral reefs, graceful sea turtles, and even a majestic manta ray gliding effortlessly through the water.

With each dive, Sophie felt more and more at home in the underwater world. She learned to control her breathing and move with ease through the water, feeling weightless and free. The colors and textures of the underwater world were unlike anything she had ever seen before, and she found herself growing more and more fascinated with each passing day.

But perhaps the most incredible experience came when Sophie encountered a pod of dolphins while out on a dive. They swam playfully around her, chattering and clicking in a way that seemed almost like conversation. Sophie couldn't help but feel a sense of awe and wonder at these intelligent creatures, and she knew that this was an experience she would never forget.

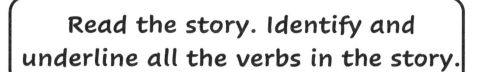

As her diving adventure ended, Sophie knew that she had experienced something truly special. The underwater world had opened to her in a way that she never thought possible, and she felt a deep connection to the sea and all the creatures that lived within it.

In the weeks and months that followed, Sophie found herself longing to return to the sea. She knew that there was still so much more to explore and discover, and she vowed to continue her underwater adventures for years to come.

For Sophie, diving into the sea had been more than just an adventure; it had been a transformational experience that had forever changed the way she looked at the world around her.

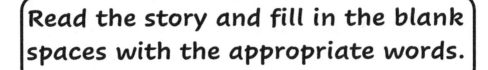

Moonwalk

- Sophie had always been fascinated by the _____ world, so she decided to embark on a scuba diving adventure to explore the sea up close and personal.
- As she geared up in her _____ and _____, she felt a thrill of excitement run through her veins.
- She was about to experience something truly _____.
- The moment she submerged into the water, Sophie was struck by the incredible _____ of the underwater world.
- Schools of fish darted around her, their _____ shimmering in the sunlight filtering down from above.
- As she swam deeper into the sea, she encountered even more incredible sights, towering _____, graceful sea _____, and even a majestic manta ray gliding effortlessly through the water.
- With each dive, Sophie felt more and more at _____ in the underwater world.
- She learned to control her _____ and move with ease through the water, feeling weightless and free.
- The colors and _____ of the underwater world were unlike anything she had ever seen before, and she found herself growing more and more fascinated with each passing day.
- But perhaps the most incredible experience came when Sophie encountered a pod of _____ while out on a dive. They swam playfully around her, chattering and clicking in a way that seemed almost like conversation.
- Sophie couldn't help but feel a sense of awe and wonder at these _____ creatures, and she knew that this was an experience she would never forget.

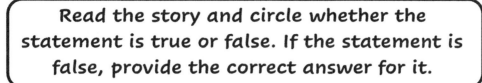

ophie has always been fascinated by the world above ground.

True   False

_____

Sophie decided to embark on a scuba diving adventure to explore the sea up close and personal.

True   False

_____

_____

_____

\s soon as she submerged into the water, Sophie was struck by the incredible beauty of the underwater world.

True   False

_____

_____

Sophie found the underwater world to be dull and uninteresting.

True   False

_____

Sophie felt a deep connection to the sea and all the creatures that lived within it.

True   False

_____

Read the story 'Diving into the deep sea' and answer the following questions.

What inspired Sophie to embark on a scuba diving adventure?

_____

_____

_____

_____

What did Sophie encounter on her dives in the sea?

_____

_____

_____

_____

How did Sophie feel about the underwater world as she explored it?

_____

_____

_____

_____

What was the most incredible experience Sophie had while scuba diving?

_____

_____

_____

_____

_____

How did Sophie feel about the sea and its creatures after her diving adventure was over?

_____

_____

_____

_____

_____

Sophie had always been fascinated by the underwater world, so she decided to embark on a scuba diving adventure to explore the sea up close and personal.	27
As she geared up in her wetsuit and tanks, she felt a thrill of excitement run through her veins. She was about to experience something truly magical.	54
The moment she submerged into the water, Sophie was struck by the incredible beauty of the underwater world.	72
Schools of fish darted around her, their scales shimmering in the sunlight filtering down from above.	89
As she swam deeper into the sea, she encountered even more incredible sights, towering coral reefs, graceful sea turtles, and even a majestic manta ray gliding effortlessly through the water.	118
With each dive, Sophie felt more and more at home in the underwater world.	132
She learned to control her breathing and move with ease through the water, feeling weightless and free.	149
The colors and textures of the underwater world were unlike anything she had ever seen before, and she found herself growing more and more fascinated with each passing day.	178
But perhaps the most incredible experience came when Sophie encountered a pod of dolphins while out on a dive.	197
They swam playfully around her, chattering and clicking in a way that seemed almost like conversation.	213
Sophie couldn't help but feel a sense of awe and wonder at these intelligent creatures, and she knew that this was an experience she would never forget.	240

As her diving adventure ended, Sophie knew that she had experienced something truly special.	254
The underwater world had opened to her in a way that she never thought possible, and she felt a deep connection to the sea and all the creatures that lived within it.	286
In the weeks and months that followed, Sophie found herself longing to return to the sea.	302
She knew that there was still so much more to explore and discover, and she vowed to continue her underwater adventures for years to come.	327
For Sophie, diving into the sea had been more than just an adventure; it had been a transformational experience that had forever changed the way she looked at the world around her.	359

Date			
Words per minute			
Number of errors			

Underwater

_____
- -
_____

World

_____
- -
_____

Turtles

_____
- -
_____

Dolphin

_____
- -
_____

Fish

_____
- -
_____

Creatures

_____
- -
_____

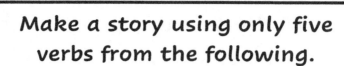

Make a story using only five verbs from the following.

found   rely   cleared   harms
contributes   protect   use
damaging   remains

_____

- -

_____

_____

- -

_____

_____

- -

_____

_____

- -

_____

_____

- -

_____

_____

- -

_____

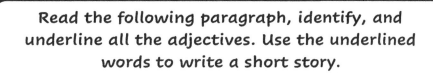

Diving into the underwater world is an adventure like no other. It's a mesmerizing experience that can be described in countless words, such as breathtaking, tranquil, mysterious, serene, fascinating, vibrant, colorful, surreal, majestic, and enchanting. As you embark on your journey beneath the waves, you're immediately immersed in a different world. The aquatic world is full of wonder, with schools of fish darting around you, curious sea turtles gliding past you, and massive manta rays soaring through the water effortlessly. The colors and textures of this new world are unlike anything you've ever seen before. The corals and sea anemones sway with the gentle currents, creating a hypnotic dance that's both mesmerizing and calming. The slow and steady rhythm of your breathing mixes with the sound of the water, creating an almost meditative atmosphere. Diving into the underwater world is a truly transformative experience that will leave you with memories that last a lifetime.

Story

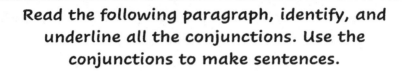

Read the following paragraph, identify, and underline all the conjunctions. Use the conjunctions to make sentences.

Diving into the underwater world can be an unforgettable experience, and it's all about being present and open to the moment. Whether you're a seasoned diver or a beginner, diving can be exciting, challenging, and awe-inspiring. When you're beneath the surface of the water, you'll see a whole new world that's both beautiful and mysterious. You might see colorful schools of fish swimming in harmony, or a graceful sea turtle gliding past you. And, as you explore further, you could come across a majestic manta ray floating effortlessly through the water. But, to fully immerse yourself in this enchanting world, you need to be patient and calm, allowing yourself to become one with the water. As you take deep breaths and slowly move through the water, you'll feel a sense of peace and tranquility that's hard to find anywhere else. In essence, diving can be a truly transformative experience – one that challenges, excites, and inspires you all at once.

Conjunctions	Sentences

83

Find and circle the words written below.

underwater   diving   sea
creatures   dolphins   coral
fish   turtles

c	r	e	a	t	u	r	e	s	c	a	n
d	c	w	a	l	k	s	q	j	e	p	e
o	o	c	s	i	s	b	p	i	s	a	a
l	r	h	t	g	o	e	g	v	e	m	l
p	a	l	a	k	c	e	j	l	i	r	g
h	l	r	r	a	i	r	k	e	c	h	n
i	f	i	s	h	e	c	r	a	f	t	i
n	t	u	r	t	l	e	s	o	n	a	v
s	m	f	i	r	s	t	r	s	s	e	i
u	n	d	e	r	w	a	t	e	r	t	d

A trip to the zoo

It was a beautiful Sunday morning, and the Johnson family decided to embark on an adventure to the local zoo. The kids, Emily and Max, were over the moon with excitement as they loaded up the car and headed towards the zoo.

As they arrived, they were greeted by the sounds of exotic animals and the smells of popcorn and cotton candy. The family quickly made their way through the entrance gate and began their tour of the zoo.

The first stop was the monkey exhibit, and the family was amazed at how playful and energetic these creatures were. Emily and Max giggled as the monkeys swung from branch to branch, showing off their acrobatic skills. They even got to see a baby monkey clinging tightly to its mother's back, which was simply adorable.

Next up was the lion exhibit, and the family was in awe of these majestic creatures. The lions lazily lounged in the sun, occasionally yawning and stretching their massive paws. Emily and Max were fascinated by their giant manes, and they couldn't help but imagine what it would be like to be that close to such powerful animals.

After the lions, the family made their way to the elephant exhibit. The elephants were enormous, towering over the family with their long trunks and majestic tusks. Emily and Max were amazed at how gentle these giants were, as they gracefully moved around their enclosure, munching on hay and interacting with their caretakers.

As the day progressed, the family explored more of the zoo and came face to face with a variety of exotic animals, including snakes, bears, tigers, and zebras. They even got to see a baby giraffe taking its first wobbly steps, which was an incredible moment.

As the sun began to set, the family made their way towards the exit, tired but happy after a long day of adventure. Emily and Max chattered excitedly about their favorite animals, and their parents couldn't help but smile at the joy on their faces.

As they drove home, the family reflected on their day at the zoo and how it brought them closer together. They vowed to make it a new tradition, and they couldn't wait for their next adventure together.

In conclusion, the trip to the zoo was an unforgettable experience for the Johnson family. It was a day filled with laughter, learning, and most importantly, spending quality time together. They left with memories that would last a lifetime and a renewed appreciation for the incredible animals that share our planet.

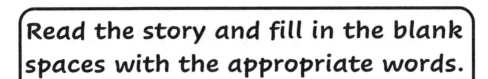

A trip to the zoo

- It was a beautiful Sunday morning, and the _____ family decided to embark on an adventure to the local zoo.
- The kids, _____ and Max, were over the moon with excitement as they loaded up the car and headed towards the zoo.
- As they arrived, they were greeted by the sounds of exotic animals and the smells of _____ and cotton candy.
- The family quickly made their way through the _____ gate and began their tour of the zoo.
- The first stop was the _____ exhibit, and the family was amazed at how playful and energetic these creatures were.
- Emily and Max giggled as the monkeys _____ from branch to branch, showing off their _____ skills.
- They even got to see a _____ clinging tightly to its mother's back, which was simply adorable.
- Next up was the _____ exhibit, and the family was in awe of these majestic creatures.
- The lions lazily lounged in the sun, occasionally yawning and stretching their massive paws. Emily and Max were fascinated by their giant _____, and they couldn't help but imagine what it would be like to be that close to such powerful animals.
- After the lions, the family made their way to the _____ exhibit.
- The elephants were enormous, towering over the family with their long _____ and majestic _____.
- Emily and Max were amazed at how gentle these giants were, as they gracefully moved around their enclosure, munching on _____ and interacting with their caretakers.

Read the story and circle whether the statement is true or false. If the statement is false, provide the correct answer for it.

The Johnson family went to the zoo on a beautiful Sunday morning.

True   False

_____

The family only saw monkeys, lions, and elephants at the zoo.

True   False

_____

The elephants at the zoo were aggressive towards the family.

True   False

_____

Emily and Max saw a baby giraffe taking its first steps.

True   False

_____

The family didn't enjoy their day at the zoo.

True   False

_____

The Johnson family made a new tradition to visit the zoo every year.

True   False

_____

The family only spent a few hours at the zoo before leaving.

True   False

_____

Read the story 'A trip to the zoo' and answer the following questions.

What animals did the family see at the zoo?

_____

_____

_____

_____

How did the family react when they saw a baby monkey clinging to its mother's back?

_____

_____

_____

_____

What was Emily and Max's favorite animal at the zoo?

_____

_____

_____

_____

_____

_____

Did the elephants at the zoo seem aggressive or gentle?

_____

_____

_____

_____

_____

What did the Johnson family reflect upon during their drive home from the zoo?

_____

_____

_____

Assess your reading fluency by writing the number of words read per minute.

It was a beautiful Sunday morning, and the Johnson family decided to embark on an adventure to the local zoo.	20
The kids, Emily and Max, were over the moon with excitement as they loaded up the car and headed towards the zoo.	42
As they arrived, they were greeted by the sounds of exotic animals and the smells of popcorn and cotton candy.	62
The family quickly made their way through the entrance gate and began their tour of the zoo.	79
The first stop was the monkey exhibit, and the family was amazed at how playful and energetic these creatures were.	99
Emily and Max giggled as the monkeys swung from branch to branch, showing off their acrobatic skills.	116
They even got to see a baby monkey clinging tightly to its mother's back, which was simply adorable.	134
Next up was the lion exhibit, and the family was in awe of these majestic creatures.	150
The lions lazily lounged in the sun, occasionally yawning and stretching their massive paws.	164
Emily and Max were fascinated by their giant manes, and they couldn't help but imagine what it would be like to be that close to such powerful animals.	192
After the lions, the family made their way to the elephant exhibit.	204
The elephants were enormous, towering over the family with their long trunks and majestic tusks.	219
Emily and Max were amazed at how gentle these giants were, as they gracefully moved around their enclosure, munching on hay and interacting with their caretakers.	245
As the day progressed, the family explored more of the zoo and came face to face with a variety of exotic animals, including snakes, bears, tigers, and zebras.	273
They even got to see a baby giraffe taking its first wobbly steps, which was an incredible moment.	291
As the sun began to set, the family made their way towards the exit, tired but happy after a long day of adventure.	314

Emily and Max chattered excitedly about their favorite animals, and their parents couldn't help but smile at the joy on their faces.	336
As they drove home, the family reflected on their day at the zoo and how it brought them closer together.	253
They vowed to make it a new tradition, and they couldn't wait for their next adventure together.	373
In conclusion, the trip to the zoo was an unforgettable experience for the Johnson family.	388
It was a day filled with laughter, learning, and most importantly, spending quality time together.	403
They left with memories that would last a lifetime and a renewed appreciation for the incredible animals that share our planet	424

Date			
Words per minute			
Number of errors			

Make sentences using the words written below.

Zoo

_____

_____

Animals

_____

_____

Elephant

_____

_____

Lion

_____

_____

Monkey

_____

_____

Zebras

_____

_____

Make a story using only five verbs from the following.

loaded   headed   arrived   greeted
made   swung   showed   giggled
lounged   yawning   stretching

_____

- -

_____

- -

_____

- -

_____

- -

_____

- -

_____

- -

_____

- -

_____

A visit to the zoo is an unforgettable and awe-inspiring experience. The animals are magnificent, and seeing them in person up-close is mesmerizing. They are majestic, gentle, playful, and energetic all at the same time. The environment is captivating and fascinating, with lush greenery, natural habitats, and exotic scents. The atmosphere is vibrant, lively, and teeming with excitement. It's a fun-filled, educational adventure that the whole family can enjoy. The experience is informative, engaging, and interactive, providing insight into the world of nature and wildlife. A trip to the zoo truly is an incredible and exhilarating experience.

Story

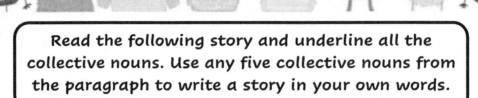

During my visit to the zoo, I was struck by the beauty and diversity of the animals. A troop of monkeys swung from branch to branch, chattering and playing with one another. A pride of lions lounged in the sun, yawning and stretching as they soaked up the warm rays. A herd of elephants moved gracefully through the park, munching on leaves and interacting with one another. A flock of colorful birds flew overhead, adding a burst of vibrancy to the scene. As I explored the various exhibits, I couldn't help but be amazed by the sheer number of species represented in one place. The zoo truly is a wonderland of wildlife.

Story

Find and circle the words written below.

zoo   lion   elephant   monkey
zebra   exhibit   animals

c	a	u	e	x	h	i	b	i	t	y	m
e	m	e	l	e	p	h	a	n	t	m	o
s	o	h	l	i	m	p	i	n	z	e	n
s	n	p	i	y	p	e	n	v	e	m	a
y	k	a	r	n	t	c	g	l	b	n	r
l	e	r	p	a	n	e	s	e	s	c	c
o	y	l	e	e	p	i	q	e	a	z	n
o	e	e	j	l	u	j	n	c	v	b	o
z	o	l	o	r	f	u	l	g	t	w	i
a	n	i	m	a	l	z	e	b	r	a	l

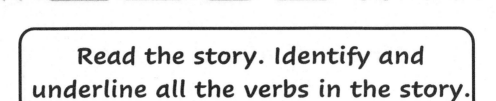

Paleontologist for a day

Lena was an eight-year-old girl, and she had always been fascinated by dinosaurs. She read books about them, watched movies about them, and even had a dinosaur-themed bedroom. So, when her parents told her they were taking her to a "Footsteps of Dinosaurs" exhibit at the local museum, she was over the moon with excitement.

The exhibit was called "Paleontologist for a Day," and it allowed children to experience what it would be like to study dinosaurs and their remains. Lena was thrilled to participate and couldn't wait to get started. The first thing they did was watch a video about the different kinds of fossils that are found and how to identify them. Lena learned that fossils are formed when plants, animals, or other organisms are buried under sediment or rock and are gradually replaced by minerals from the ground.

After the video, Lena and her family were taken to a mock excavation site where they could dig and uncover dinosaur bones. They were given shovels, brushes, and buckets and were allowed to excavate as much as they wanted. Lena felt like a true paleontologist, brushing away dirt to reveal the bones of a Tyrannosaurus Rex. She was amazed by how big and heavy the bones were.

Next, Lena and her family were brought to a lab where they learned how scientists use various tools to study fossils. They got to examine different types of bones under microscopes and magnifying glasses and learn how to identify them. The instructors showed them how to measure the bones, analyze their structure, and make educated guesses about the kind of animal they belonged to.

Read the story. Identify and underline all the verbs in the story.

Finally, Lena's favorite part came creating her own dinosaur. She was given a blank silhouette of a dinosaur and was allowed to attach any features she wanted. She chose a long neck, sharp teeth, and a spiky tail. Her imagination went wild, and she drew a dinosaur that was both terrifying and fascinating.

The "Paleontologist for a Day" exhibit was an incredible experience for Lena and her family. It taught them about the science of paleontology, how fossils are studied, and what it's like to be a paleontologist. Lena left the exhibit with a newfound appreciation for dinosaurs and the people who study them. She knew that she wanted to learn even more about these fascinating creatures and maybe even become a paleontologist herself one day.

Paleontologist for a day

- _____ was an eight-year-old girl, and she had always been fascinated by dinosaurs.
- She read books about them, watched movies about them, and even had a _____-themed bedroom.
- So, when her parents told her they were taking her to a "_____" exhibit at the local museum, she was over the moon with excitement.
- The exhibit was called "_____," and it allowed children to experience what it would be like to study dinosaurs and their remains.
- Lena was thrilled to _____ and couldn't wait to get started.
- The first thing they did was watch a video about the different kinds of _____ that are found and how to identify them.
- Lena learned that fossils are formed when _____, _____, or other organisms are buried under sediment or rock and are gradually replaced by minerals from the ground.
- After the video, Lena and her family were taken to a _____ excavation site where they could dig and uncover dinosaur bones.
- They were given _____, _____, and buckets and were allowed to excavate as much as they wanted.
- Lena felt like a true _____, brushing away dirt to reveal the bones of a _____ _____.
- She was amazed by how big and heavy the _____ were.
- Next, Lena and her family were brought to a _____ where they learned how scientists use various tools to study fossils.

Lena has always been fascinated by dinosaurs.

True   False

_____

The exhibit that Lena visited was called "Journey to the Moon".

True   False

_____

Lena got to excavate dinosaur bones at a mock excavation site.

True   False

_____

Lena learned about how fossils are formed during the exhibit.

True   False

_____

Lena did not get to create her own dinosaur during the exhibit.

True   False

_____

The instructors showed Lena and her family how to measure the bones and analyze their structure.

True   False

_____

Read the story 'Paleontologist for a day' and answer the following questions.

What exhibit did Lena's parents take her to at the local museum?

_____

_____

_____

_____

What did Lena learn about how fossils are formed?

_____

_____

_____

_____

What tools did Lena and her family use to study fossils in the lab?

_____

_____

_____

_____

_____

_____

_____

What did Lena leave the exhibit with?

_____

_____

_____

_____

_____

_____

What was Lena's favorite part of the "Paleontologist for a Day" exhibit?

_____

_____

_____

_____

Lena was an eight-year-old girl, and she had always been fascinated by dinosaurs.	13
She read books about them, watched movies about them, and even had a dinosaur-themed bedroom.	28
So, when her parents told her they were taking her to a "Footsteps of Dinosaurs" exhibit at the local museum, she was over the moon with excitement.	55
The exhibit was called "Paleontologist for a Day," and it allowed children to experience what it would be like to study dinosaurs and their remains.	80
Lena was thrilled to participate and couldn't wait to get started.	91
The first thing they did was watch a video about the different kinds of fossils that are found and how to identify them.	114
Lena learned that fossils are formed when plants, animals, or other organisms are buried under sediment or rock and are gradually replaced by minerals from the ground.	141
After the video, Lena and her family were taken to a mock excavation site where they could dig and uncover dinosaur bones.	163
They were given shovels, brushes, and buckets and were allowed to excavate as much as they wanted.	180
Lena felt like a true paleontologist, brushing away dirt to reveal the bones of a Tyrannosaurus Rex. She was amazed by how big and heavy the bones were.	208
Next, Lena and her family were brought to a lab where they learned how scientists use various tools to study fossils.	229
They got to examine different types of bones under microscopes and magnifying glasses and learn how to identify them.	248

The instructors showed them how to measure the bones, analyze their structure, and make educated guesses about the kind of animal they belonged to Finally, Lena's favorite part came creating her own dinosaur.	281
She was given a blank silhouette of a dinosaur and was allowed to attach any features she wanted.	299
She chose a long neck, sharp teeth, and a spiky tail. Her imagination went wild, and she drew a dinosaur that was both terrifying and fascinating.	325
The "Paleontologist for a Day" exhibit was an incredible experience for Lena and her family.	340
It taught them about the science of paleontology, how fossils are studied, and what it's like to be a paleontologist.	361
Lena left the exhibit with a newfound appreciation for dinosaurs and the people who study them.	376
She knew that she wanted to learn even more about these fascinating creatures and maybe even become a paleontologist herself one day.	398

Date			
Words per minute			
Number of errors			

Paleontologist

_____

_____

Dinosaur

_____

_____

Ancient

_____

_____

Discover

_____

_____

Shovel

_____

_____

Brushes

_____

_____

Make a story using only five
verbs from the following.

had been   fascinated   read   watched

took   participating   started   watch

learned   formed   buried   replaced

_____
- -
_____
- -
_____
- -
_____
- -
_____
- -
_____
- -
_____
- -
_____
- -
_____
- -

Read the following story and underline all the adjectives. Use any five adjectives from the paragraph to write a story in your own words.

Dinosaurs are fascinating, prehistoric creatures that roamed the earth millions of years ago. They were colossal, intimidating, and awe-inspiring, with sharp teeth, massive bodies, and powerful limbs. They were ferocious, but also gentle, nurturing, and intelligent, with complex social structures and habits. The world they lived in was lush, tropical, and teeming with life, and they ruled it with an unmatched prowess. Their existence is shrouded in mystery, but their impact on the planet is undeniable - they shaped the landscape and ecosystem, and their legacy continues to captivate and inspire people of all ages.

Story

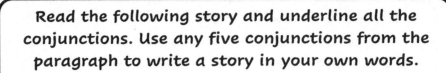

Read the following story and underline all the conjunctions. Use any five conjunctions from the paragraph to write a story in your own words.

Dinosaurs are fascinating creatures that have captured the imagination of people for generations, and it's easy to see why. They were colossal and awe-inspiring, with sharp teeth, massive bodies, and powerful limbs, yet they were also gentle and nurturing. They lived in a world that was lush, tropical, and teeming with life, and they ruled it with an unmatched prowess. Although their existence is shrouded in mystery, their impact on the planet is undeniable. From shaping the landscape and ecosystem to inspiring people of all ages, dinosaurs have left an indelible mark on history, and their legacy continues to endure.

Story

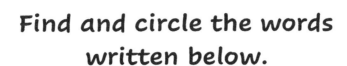

Find and circle the words written below.

dinosaurs   fascinate   explore
shovel   dig   brush

h	e	x	p	l	o	r	e	k	f	y	d
e	s	f	i	m	k	k	w	j	a	m	e
s	h	h	l	i	m	p	i	n	w	e	t
f	o	r	e	g	t	e	n	v	n	m	a
y	v	a	i	n	t	c	g	l	b	n	n
l	e	d	p	b	r	u	s	h	s	c	i
a	l	a	z	i	n	g	s	e	a	z	c
s	e	e	j	l	u	j	e	c	v	b	s
c	o	l	o	r	f	u	e	g	t	w	a
d	i	n	o	s	a	u	r	s	i	t	f

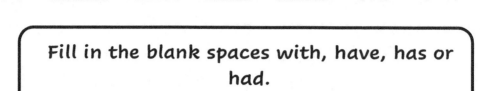

Fill in the blank spaces with, have, has or had.

1. He _____ a collection of rare stamps from around the world.

2. We _____ been to that restaurant before, and the food was delicious.

3. She _____ a terrible headache yesterday, but she's feeling much better today.

4. They _____ been planning their vacation for months and are excited to finally go.

5. The company _____ recently introduced a new product line.

6. I _____ never seen that movie before, but I've heard it's really good.

7. The teacher _____ to grade a stack of papers over the weekend.

8. He _____ a lot of experience in the field and is considered an expert.

9. We _____ a great time at the party last night.

10. The team _____ been practicing hard and is ready for the big game.

1. I want to go to the beach, but it's too cold outside.

2. She likes to read books and watch movies on the weekends.

3. You can have a slice of cake as long as you finish your dinner first.

4. He ran in the park even though it was raining.

5. We went to the concert, yet we missed the opening act.

6. She studied hard all semester, so she got good grades on her exams.

7. The dog barked loudly because he was scared of the thunderstorm.

8. He wants to go on vacation either to Hawaii or to the Caribbean.

9. They finished building the house before the deadline, but it was over budget.

10. She is a talented musician, but she is also a great athlete.

Use the following words into your own sentences.

For   and   nor   but   or   yet   so   after   although   as

Read the sentences and underline the pronouns in each sentence.

1. I want to go to the beach, but it's too cold outside.

2. She likes to read books and watch movies on the weekends.

3. You can have a slice of cake as long as you finish your dinner first.

4. He ran in the park even though it was raining.

5. We went to the concert, yet we missed the opening act.

6. She studied hard all semester, so she got good grades on her exams.

7. The dog barked loudly because he feared the thunderstorm.

8. He wants to go on vacation either to Hawaii or to the Caribbean.

9. They finished building the house before the deadline, but it was over budget.

Change the following sentences into interrogative sentences.

1. He is going to the store to buy milk.

2. She likes to read books in her free time.

3. They will be leaving for vacation next week.

4. He went to the gym this morning.

5. The dog barks loudly at strangers.

6. She is a talented musician.

7. We were happy with the service at the restaurant.

8. They have been planning their wedding for months.

Look at the picture. Write five sentences in interrogative way by looking at the picture.

Look at the picture. Write five compound sentences by looking at the picture.

Made in the USA
Las Vegas, NV
01 March 2024

86494158R00070